LEDISI
Better Than Alright
Finding
PEACE
LOVE&
POWER

ESSENCE

Editor-in-Chief: Constance C.R. White
Executive Editor: Vanessa K. Bush
Creative Director: Greg Monfries
Managing Editor: Michael Q. Bullerdick
Editorial Production Manager: LaToya N. Valmont

ESSENCE PRESENTS
LEDISI: BETTER THAN ALRIGHT
FINDING PEACE, LOVE & POWER

Editor: Patrik Henry Bass
Art Director: Sandy Lawrence
Photo Editor: Leah Rudulfo
Copy Editor: Hope Wright
Imaging Specialist: Kevin Grimstead

Publisher: Richard Fraiman
Vice President, Business Development & Strategy:
Steven Sandonato
Executive Director, Marketing Services:
Carol Pittard
Executive Director, Retail & Special Sales:
Tom Mifsud
Executive Director, New Product Development:
Peter Harper
Editorial Director: Stephen Koepp
Director, Bookazine Development & Marketing:
Laura Adam
Publishing Director: Joy Butts
Finance Director: Glenn Buonocore
Assistant General Counsel: Helen Wan
Assistant Director, Special Sales: Ilene Schreider
Book Production Manager: Susan Chodakiewicz
Design & Prepress Manager: Anne-Michelle Gallero
Brand Manager: Roshni Patel

Special Thanks:
Christine Austin, Jeremy Biloon,
Denolyn Carroll, Jim Childs, Rose Cirrincione,
Lauren Hall Clark, Sherrill Clarke, Pinda D. Romain,
Jacqueline Fitzgerald, Carrie Hertan, Christine Font,
Jenna Goldberg, Hillary Hirsch, Suzanne Janso,
Amy Mangus, Robert Marasco, Kimberly Marshall,
Amy Migliaccio, Nina Mistry, Dave Rozzelle,
Adriana Tierno, Alex Voznesenskiy,
Grace White, Tracey Woods, Vanessa Wu

Copyright © 2012
Time Home Entertainment, Inc.

Published by ESSENCE Books, an imprint of
Time Home Entertainment, Inc.
135 W. 50th St.
New York NY 10020

ISBN 10: 1-60320-182-3
ISBN 13: 978-1-60320-182-7
Library of Congress Control Number: 2012931898

Printed in China

We welcome your comments and suggestions about
ESSENCE Books. Please write to us at:
ESSENCE Books
Attention: Book Editors
P.O. Box 11016
Des Moines IA 50336-1016

If you would like to order any of our hardcover
Collector's Edition books, please call us at
800-327-6388 (Monday through Friday,
7:00 A.M.–8:00 P.M., or Saturday, 7:00 A.M.–6:00 P.M.
Central Standard Time).

Contents

Dedication

For you, Mama...love you forever and past that NyDy.

Acknowledgments

Thank you, God, for my life and for words. Thank you Daddy for always reminding me to put God first. I wish we'd had more time. I love you so much. R.I.P. Thank you, Lorenzo, for encouraging me to be clear. Never try—do it! Thank you to my sisters, Shannon and Tamyra, for being the greatest inspiration in the world. Thank you to my best friend Kenyatte for being my eyes when I can't see things clearly. Thank you, Cecile Thalley, for pushing me to finish. You are an incredible friend. Thank God for you!

Thank you, Iya, Baba Skip, Rex, Xavier, Kim, Cora, Marie, Lorena, Troy, Roland, Matthew, Sara, Clyde and Wanda, for being there every part of my journey. I love you all.

Thank you, Rachelle Ferrell, Chaka Khan, Ms. Patti, Mr. Prince, Stevie, Ms. Anita Baker and Ms. Aretha Franklin, for embracing me. Thank for just being you. I love you all so much. Wow! Thank you.

Thank you, President Barack Obama, Mrs. Michelle Obama, Bishop T.D. Jakes, Dr. Maya Angelou and Iyanla Vanzant, for your words. Through your books and your words of encouragement, you have helped me become a better writer, person and woman. [*Hands lifted*] Thank you! Thank you for seeing me!

Thank you to Peter, Patrik, Constance, Stephanie, LaToya, Hope, Leah, Sandy, Kevin and everyone at ESSENCE/Time Warner, Inc., for working so hard on my vision and believing in me. This is beyond what I imagined. Please! Can we do it again? Thank you, Joi Rideout. Love you, sis! Thank you, Benchmark Entertainment (John Dee and Kevin Gasser), Safe Haven (Roland Jack), Gray Krauss Stratford Des Rochers, LLP (Evan Krauss), and Deblois Meja and Kaplan, LLP (Mark Kaplan)—my wonderful team—for taking care of everything. This is truly another dream come true.

Thank you to all of my fans (like-minded spirits) and anyone who supports this book. I pray that it will inspire you to always choose love and be "better than alright!" [*Laughing*] Dear Life...I wouldn't change a thing. Well...maybe one thing. [*Laughing*] Yes, God! I AM!!! Thank you!

Introduction

I'll never forget the first time I saw the lavish coffee-table book *ESSENCE: 25 Years of Celebrating Black Women*, featuring the elegant model Mounia fearlessly staring as if to say, "The world is ours." This sumptuous and colorful silver anniversary tribute, which showcased phenomenal celebrities, activists, authors, lawmakers, executives and entrepreneurs, was one of our first publishing efforts. Over the years, we've added books about spirituality, beauty and wellness, along with our best-selling titles on the First Family, to your bookshelf. Now I'm pleased to share with you our latest offering, *Better Than Alright: Finding Peace, Love & Power* by the extraordinary singer Ledisi.

Beautiful, talented, sexy, smart, original, funny and soulful, Ledisi embodies the modern ESSENCE woman. We first heard about her in 2008, when she appeared at our annual Black Women in Hollywood Luncheon and had everyone standing on their feet with her soaring rendition of The Beatles' classic "Yesterday."

Ledisi was on her way, and ESSENCE was a critical part of her journey. Little did we know that her writing voice was as powerful as her singing voice. A little over two years ago, ESSENCE Finance and Operations Director Stephanie Perry heard that Ledisi was interested in penning a book.

Stephanie reached out to Peter Harper, our former publishing partner at Time Home Entertainment, Inc., and ESSENCE Senior Editor Patrik Henry Bass. They took a look at Ledisi's poetic and insightful work and thought that not only was there a book, but there was inspiration and celebration of who we are and what we love.

Ledisi wrote through the recording of four albums, and while traveling across several continents. *Better Than Alright*, a moving collection of essays, songs, poems and quotes by the singer, charts her path to inner peace, personal power and purpose.

We've designed this special book for you to carry in your purse on your own journey. We know you're the driver in your life and we hope that you will allow us to come along for an extraordinary ride on this trip called life.

CONSTANCE C.R. WHITE
Editor-in-Chief

The Journey

Wow...every time I look at what I have written, I become overwhelmed with joy. I can't believe someone found my journey interesting enough to want to put it in a book. (((((Hug))))) Please consider that a hug from me to you. (((((Laughing)))))

You know, being on display as an artist is never comfortable for me. Behind my songs and my words lies a very shy little girl who has become a strong woman. Luckily, there are people around me who push and lift me to be open and transparent. Over and over, I would hear the phrase "tell the story." My vocal coach, teachers, mother, friends and mentors would say, "Just tell the story, Ledisi." I'll never forget the day I was in the conference room with Patrik, my editor, and he repeated the phrase as if it were God reminding me of his presence, "Ledisi, all you have to do is tell the story."

So here I am, and in every chapter of this book are fragments of my life between the lines and spaces of music. Pivotal moments that are filled with ups and downs, challenges and triumphs. Experiences that shaped the woman and the singer you have come to know as Ledisi.

The first chapter is a big part of my journey, and I purposely displayed each moment in the order in which each experience happened. As you read this, I hope you will be on the journey with me to see how one moment prepared me for the next. Oh, what a journey!

I learned everything is connected and everything happens for a reason. The answer may not come right away, but be certain the answer will come. It always comes right on time. (((((Laughing))))) The true lesson for me was recognizing the lesson. Some of us do not always use the gift of awareness. I hope you will be inspired by my journey. The gift of life is bigger than all of us, and I have come to know my soul is truly anchored by God to "tell the story."

All of this has led me to this!

hey, you

Have you stopped to take a breath?
Have you looked at what's now instead of what's next?
Breathe
Close your eyes
Remember
It's bigger than you
Bigger than all of this
Hey! There's more beyond here and more things you may fear
But focus on now
Don't miss the now
This is it!
When tomorrow comes, you'll want to say,
"Wow! Yesterday was extraordinary"
Hey, you!
Don't miss the now worrying about yesterday

The essence of life

 ne of the most amazing experiences in my life was when I was invited to sing at the first annual ESSENCE Black Women in Hollywood Luncheon. This was my first time being invited to a star-studded event. On the drive from the airport, I looked out the window at the palm trees and the fancy cars that breezed past my limo. I couldn't help but notice the many labels that were every-where around me. From the cars to the older ladies in their Chanel jackets to the younger women in Michael Kors shades carrying Louis Vuitton purses. The weather was beautiful and everything looked like a magazine ad.

As my car pulled into the driveway of the historic Beverly Hills Hotel, I was amazed by the immaculate landscape of the grounds. If ever there was a Hollywood moment, this was that moment for me. An ESSENCE representative greeted me with the key to my room and a bellman took my bags up. I tried to act as if I had been somewhere be-fore, but my jeans and T-shirt definitely gave me away. Not to mention that I was wide-eyed as I looked around at everything I had previously seen only in the movies. I saw famous people zoom by me with their handlers, racing down beautiful stairways. The men in tailored suits and women in Prada high heels. I got lost in the high-end cologne and fresh flowers. The decor was breathtaking and I could see all the stories this building held. I soaked it all in and felt out of place. It kind of felt like I was on a movie set and I was walking around in the way. "Ms. Young, here is your room and your bags are in the closet. If you need anything, please do not hesitate to call." If the bellman had not spoken to me, I would not have remembered that I was asked to be here and I was a guest at The Beverly Hills Hotel. I felt so honored. The light in the room danced on my face and begged me to open a window and feel the slight breeze that made the chiffon curtains flow into my room. I said a small prayer, thanking God for this little moment. I sat in silence and listened to the murmur of people talking and the birds chirping in the trees. Before I knew it, I was at the luncheon singing "Yesterday" by The Beatles. I received a standing ovation. Will and Jada Smith and Tom and Katie Cruise stood up right in front of me. I had to take a deep breath. I was honored to be in a room filled with so many people I admired. Jada Pinkett Smith was the last to be honored and Will's adoration for his wife had us all in tears. He cried and expressed his love for his wife and how much she does for him and their family while sustaining her career. I was so proud of them. They inspired love and dedication to family first as well as a strong bond with their friends. When the luncheon ended, it felt as if we had all shared something that we would never forget for the rest of our lives. We took pictures with everyone afterward and hugged one another. Tom and Katie told me they loved my performance and took a photo with me. I walked back to my room and looked out the window and thought to myself, *Wow...and this is only the beginning*. And it was the beginning of many more events but never anything like this book project. It's funny. When I see some of the women who attended that event, we always talk about how incredible that luncheon was and how you had to be there to feel what we felt. It was a spiritual connection we had all made. I will never forget that day. It was the introduction to a new level of my life. What a way to begin.

CHAPTER 1

I am not the Greatest...
God is

My talks with God

The voices and opinions of others should be an afterthought. That is why I always write/sing about the world.

Most of the time, my talks with God are through my surroundings. When I was a child, my mother introduced me to the teachings of Mother Nature. That is why I always write/sing about the world, the sun, the rain, love and the sky. I feel we are connected to everything around us.

Take time to notice those beautiful gifts. All the answers we need are right there. I say that because the best conversations happen when you are ALONE... being still. The voices and opinions of others should be an afterthought. I learned that from my talks with God. I will be taken care of...even the things I don't know are headed my way, God will take care of them all. I leave that space of solitude renewed.

Seeds of faith are always within us;
sometimes it takes a crisis to nourish
and encourage their growth.

—Susan L. Taylor

hey, you…

There is so much beauty in the simple things.
I think the more simple things are, the
better quality of life you have.
There's so much space when things are simple.

Faith is taking the first step even when you don't see the whole staircase.

—Martin Luther King, Jr.

Don't wait around for other people to be happy for you.

Any happiness you get you've got to make yourself.
—Alice Walker

Walk Around Heaven All Day

One of these mornings
Won't be very long
You're gonna look for me and I'll be gone
I'm going to a place where I'll have nothing, nothing to do
But we'll just walk around, walk around heaven all day
When I get to heaven
I'm gonna sing and shout
And nobody there will be able to put me out
My mother will be waiting
And my father, too
And we'll just walk around, walk around heaven all day
Dear Lord up above, don't you hear me praying?
Walk right by my side
Hold my hand when my way gets a little cloudy
I need you, I need you to be my guide
Every day will be Sunday, my Lord
Sabbath will have no end
And we'll do nothing but sing and praise Him
Then He'll say, "Well done"
And my race, my race will be won
And I'll walk around, walk around heaven all day
Walk around heaven
I'll just walk around heaven all day

—Cassietta George

When a person really desires something, all the universe conspires to help that person to realize his dream.

God Made Things I Love

The way my mother says, "Love you, baby"
When Shannon's about to do the happy cry
When Jessi dances
When Tamyra smiles
The way my boyfriend plays the organ
The colors blue, orange, yellow and red
Iya's love
Baba Skip's honesty
Prince's hands and his facial expressions when he's playing the guitar
The way Stevie Wonder sings
Michelle Obama's hugs
President Obama's laugh
The way Bettye LaVette sings the blues
Robert Glasper when he solos on a grand piano
Maxwell's falsetto
Esperanza Spalding when she scats and plays her bass at the same time
Chaka Khan when she poses for a picture
Aretha's low growl that moves up into a high note
When Quincy Jones looks over his glasses
My manager's eyes when he's about to tell me something funny
My other manager's face when I do something good
My friend Cee's writing
When Matt sings
When Kendall paints
The way Rex looks at his family, especially his wife, Joi
Roland's face when Al Green or Lil Wayne comes on
When Trombone Shorty and Kermit Ruffin play together

The sky in any part of Africa
A full moon
The sky in New Orleans
When the audience sings along
The way words are used and misused
Tina Turner's legs
Oprah Winfrey and Iyanla Vanzant
Fried tilapia
Being on time
Music
Fruit in Hawaii
Jordy playing guitar
Josh when he calls me "Auntie"
The ocean
Belief
When DuRon cooks
Ella Fitzgerald's voice
Marvin Gaye's voice and wiggle
Blood red oranges
French fries
Kenyatte
Mango pineapple smoothies
Blue people
Black people
White people
Brown people
All people
Apple Now and Laters

My faith has brought me through...

_____

_____

_____

_____

_____

_____

_____

I believe...

_____

_____

_____

_____

_____

_____

_____

My talks with God

(Draw or place your visuals here)

CHAPTER 2

BEAUTY

I cannot accept the
way things are because
I can see how
much more
beautiful
things could be

Writing "Pieces of Me"

I remember feeling so overwhelmed toward the end of making my album *Pieces of Me*. I was having a bad day, ready to hide away from the world. Everything was happening so fast and all at the same time. I wanted to be excited, but everything depended on me making things happen. There's so much pressure that goes with making an album. I had not eaten and was feeling extremely bloated and ugly. [*Laughing*] I was having a woman kind of day. This was my final weekend of sessions, and today the producers would be Chuck Harmony and Claude Kelly. It was going to be my first time working with Chuck Harmony, and all I wanted to do was be in bed reading a book. I didn't want to sing. When I finally made it to the studio, Chuck had headphones on while pounding on a keyboard and Claude was sitting on a sofa smiling at me with his laptop in his lap.

Sweaty from the hot L.A. sun and filled with great anxiety from the pressure to produce a hit album, I reluctantly sat down next to Claude. I had my bag of food from Boston Market filled with vegetables and sweet potatoes. Chuck unplugged his headphones and the track began to play. At first, I thought, *It's alright. Not something I would normally sing against. But hey, I haven't eaten and I am tired, so I can't hear nothing right now.* Claude was in heaven. He heard what I could not hear yet. Claude looked at me and said, "So, what do you think?" I said, "I like it, but I'm not sure what to say over it yet. Hi, Chuck! I'm Ledisi." Claude thought we had worked together before, but we hadn't. If you've ever seen Chuck's smile, it's incredible. He's also very quiet if he doesn't know you. No words escaped his lips, but he gave me a big hug and I shared my food with him. He was hungry too—he ate all of my sweet potatoes. So this is how I was greeted by Chuck Harmony, eating my sweet potatoes. [*Laughing*] After a while, Chuck left the room and Claude and I began to talk. "So tell me, how are you feeling right now? You're almost done. Are you excited? Talk to me," Claude said.

I wanted to run from his excitement. I pleaded with myself silently to enjoy this process and come out with a great song. I began to tell him the truth about my anxiety and how overwhelmed I was. I told him how hard I had worked and this was probably one of my best projects. It shows all the different pieces of me that I wanted people to see. He smiled and said, "Great! That is what we will talk about on this song." Then he asked the engineer to play the track, and he sang the new chorus, "pieces of me."

I was so tired vocally, mentally and spiritually, but Claude was not letting up. As the track played over and over, I began to fall in love with it—it reminded me of a church hymn. I told Claude people don't know who I am. They don't know what's behind my smile or who I am as a person. I'm like every woman: complex, sexy and sensitive. We began to write about me. Then it was my turn to lay down the vocals. I sang the song. The toughest time was with the bridge. After a while, I wanted to give up. But Claude Kelly never gave up: "Come on, Ledisi. You can do this!" Exhausted by every second, I saw that the end was finally near. I sang, "I'm a woman. These are the pieces of me." We were all silent. When that happens after a song, you know it's good. We played it back and everyone was happy, including me. Finally, I had a song that described my insecurities as well as my joy. There is so much in this song, yet it sounds so simple. In actuality, it's an incredibly hard song to sing. It wears me out every time I sing it.

I began to tell him the truth about my anxiety and how overwhelmed I was.

You So Black and Ugly

I didn't know
I was looked at
as black and ugly
until someone
told me
I was.

When I was little,
Mama would rub
cocoa butter on my legs
and tell me
how beautiful I am.

She would say,
"Look at your big, beautiful brown eyes.
Stay off your knees.
Don't ruin your beautiful legs.
You are my pretty chocolate chile."

I am not ugly.
Ugly is You calling me Ugly.

Beauty Skin-Deep

On the outside, the seams are perfectly sown,
  hair just right and teeth pearly white.
Skin smooth and flawless.
Body sculpted from the heavens.
We stare as she passes by.
We are in disbelief, men are in awe
  and women are jealous.
How could something so beautiful exist?
She knows it in the way she walks.
And she seems secure, confident and beautiful.
But if you look closely at the cracks that lie skin-
  deep, you will see a tormented soul living on
  love just like the rest of us.
Wanting love that goes far deeper than the
  shallow exterior that is only skin-deep.

Black Woman

I was made from the rib of a man
Mixed with more than grains of sand
And out of the dust I rose
Giving birth to what the future holds
Lips sweet yet my words divine
My king in front and I lead from behind
Wearing pants in the day and a garter at night
A kiss on the face, I'm the giver of life
I'm a Black Woman
A Black Woman
A Black Woman
A Black Woman

There's a child that's here in my womb
Dreaming 'bout the stars and the moon
You're my future, I hold you tight
You're my gift from God's ray of light
I'm your water, I'm your everything
I'm the strength in the air that you breathe
I'm a healer, I'm a dreamer, I am all these things
But the one gift God has given to me is
I'm a Black Woman

A Black Woman
A Black Woman
A Black Woman

My heart is giving and it's endless and it's pure as gold
Even in the days when I was bought and sold
My beauty consumes and tames the wondering mind
Darker my skin, my love's sweeter than honey wine
My kisses, my prayers will guide you to all your dreams
And when I'm loving you, I'm giving everything
I'm giving everything, everything, everything
'Cause I'm a Black Woman
A Strong Woman
A Black Woman
A Black Woman

Black, Brown, Dark Brown, High Yella, Yellow, Redbone,
Red, Caramel, Blue Black, Butterscotch, Taupe, White or
Vanilla Bean...So Mean...Love me, Love My Skin, Love the
Skin I'm In, I Am...After We Get Past All That...I Am Simply
a Woman
—*Loudspeaker Ledisi Young and X. Mosley*

Mama Song

She had tight hip-huggers on and brown high-heel shoes
  under her bell-bottom jeans
The crowd screams louder when she danced like a ballerina
  with her big Afro
She didn't have to speak
Her body spoke for her
Her smile felt good and her necklace lay on her flat tummy
  like a curtain not nearly hiding what my stepfather wanted
  no one else to see
She knew it and remained gracefully defiant
She would do things to remind him of her greatness
And he wanted to tame her, own her little spirit
Any shine that would come her way, he did everything to dim her light
But she kept on singing
Behind her song, she was raising three children, going to night school
  and battling an abusive alcoholic husband that rivaled Ike Turner
She sang and she sang and the crowd threw money
The mic could not hold her power
It had a slight distortion, but you could still feel her tone and
  the emotion in her voice
Just like her life, a bit of distortion
But it didn't stop her from expressing herself
She captivated me like a kite in the sky
Only thing would bring her down would be the person who held the strings
  to her heart
He was the evil at the end of her heartstrings, always bringing her down
But through that, she still taught me to always fly
She would whisper in my ear, "Fly, my beautiful

baby girl. Don't let no man, nobody stop you from flying"

I whispered to her, "Don't let no man, nobody stop you from flying, Mama. I gotcha, Mama. Sing your song"

I remember when her wings were so broken

I had to show her how to fly again

I had to tell her about the stories she had told me

I had to teach her how to sing again

And look at us now, singing...singing...singing

I remember when he had conquered her spirit and her wings were broken

I had to go out into the world and come back into her dysfunction and show her how to fly again

I reminded her of her words and held up the mirror she gave me

And she saw herself and she put herself together again

And she began to dance and I helped her find her voice again

I had to teach her how to sing again

And look at us now, singing and dancing and singing

I got my song and she got her song

Mama got her own song again

I whispered to her, "Don't let no man, nobody stop you from flying, Mama. I gotcha, Mama. Sing your song"

When you don't know how
beautiful you are
You will always be in search
of happiness

The most beautiful thing in the world is...

_____

_____

_____

_____

_____

_____

_____

The beautiful things about me are...

_____

_____

_____

_____

_____

_____

_____

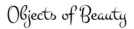

Objects of Beauty

(Draw or place your visuals here)

CHAPTER 3

LOVE

Love is at the
root of everything

y name was a sore spot for me when I was little. I was called Le-dee-see by my teachers every day. I was called Lettuce, along with many other variations of my name that were not pleasant, by the students. I hated my name. I wished it were something more simple, like Sarah or Maria. I mostly hated the way my stepfather called my name. It was the scariest sound and whenever he said it, I always knew I was in trouble for something I didn't do.

As I got older, I finally had the courage to ask my mother, "Why did you name me Ledisi?" She said: "Everything is in your name. There is so much power in your name. Did you know that you were born prematurely and the doctors said you might not make it? But you did, and the only way they kept you alive was by feeding you through a tube in your head. Then someone coughed on you when you were a little baby and you developed a spot on your lung. You almost died. You also had a crooked leg and they wanted to cut it off, but I told them to put a brace on it.

"Your name means 'to bring forth.' Your daddy named you after a Yoruba song that he heard me sing. He loved the sound of it and that became your name, Ledisi! You have been fighting to come forth ever since you were a little baby. Be proud of your name, no matter who teases you about it. They'll say it right one day, and they will remember it. Why? Because not many have a name like yours. God named you, and don't you forget it."

God named me

Soul Mates

We talk but do not speak
We listen without words
We know without thinking about it
We feel without touch
We give carefully taking
When we finally speak
We are pleasing our ears
Feeling with clear hearts and
gazing with clear minds
It's easy to synchronize
Because we are Soul Mates

LOVE Questions

Did you hear that?
"I love you."
Did you feel that?
My heartbeat
After all these years
You still make me shy
Did you see that?
The smile on my face
The smile on your face
Do you love that?
Our private conversations
Don't cha just love that?
We are beyond words
Yes, we are beyond words
You know what?
I need you
You know why?
You define Love

༄

I love when he

Sleeps

Smiles

Loves me without makeup

Pushes me to be my best

Never lets me settle

Talks to my mother

Loves his family

Hides in the background

Doesn't get too upset when

I push him to the front

Is never intimidated by my shine

Makes me laugh

Introduces me to different music

Knows when I am sad and wants to fix it

Protects us

Never lets me go

Gets on my nerves

Is strong when I am weak

Smiles

Vulnerable

Fearless

Is persistent

Takes care of me

Doesn't stay mad too long

Says, "I'm proud of you"

Does his own thing

Forgives me

Loves me

Loves me

As is

And it shows

Love   Is   Real When...

When love is real it needs   no explanation. It's clear and in full bloom, like the first day of spring. There is no uncertainty or hidden insecurities. There is just, "Here I am; here is everything I have to offer. Here is my mind, body and soul. I'm ready to receive and exchange this love. Here is my willingness to learn with you." When love is real, there are realistic views of our imperfections. And those imperfections are nurtured, greeted with warmth and enthusiasm. Let's just exist in our space in the world. Hugs are long; lips are kissed. Physical reminders of our bond. A commit-ment endless, bright like the orange rays in the sun. Actions seen in full view. Words expressed, no matter how uncomfortable or comfortable the moment may be. When love is real, it is a reflection of God's Love. The beauty of real love is that it lasts from one world to the next. And yes, Real Love lasts forever and ever and ever.

What I love about me is...

_____

_____

_____

_____

_____

_____

_____

When I think of love, I...

_____

_____

_____

_____

_____

_____

_____

_____

Share the Love

(Draw or place your visuals here)

Who makes me smile?

_____

_____

_____

_____

_____

_____

_____

_____

My objects of desire are...

_____

_____

_____

_____

_____

_____

_____

Write a love letter to yourself:

_____

_____

_____

_____

_____

_____

_____

_____

_____

_____

_____

_____

_____

_____

_____

_____

_____

_____

_____

_____

CHAPTER 4

SHINE

I Dream...
But after that,
I Live

The blue chest

When I was little, my younger sister and I used our imagination when we couldn't go outside to play. We lived in the projects, a place where I witnessed a son shoot his father while I was riding on my Big Wheel bike. Men would fight after every basketball game in the neighborhood park, and a gun would always appear out of the blue. Mama went to work during the day and to school at night. She was the provider in our family, while my stepfather played drums and took odd jobs around town. When we would come home from school, my stepfather did not want us going outside. I had already witnessed too much, and they were worried about the effect those things had on me. So while locked in our rooms like prisoners, we created a world of our own.

In the closet was a blue chest. Funny, I never opened that chest to see what was in it, but I loved that thing. The blue chest sat on the floor of the closet, which had curtains as a door, so we turned the chest into a stage. This was where I would perform in front of my audience. I used a wooden ruler for my microphone, and I would steal my mother's big shades, high heels and jewelry to create my character. I wanted to impress my fans because they had sold out my show. My audience consisted of a bunch of stuffed animals, baby dolls and my little sister sitting in the middle.

Elton John's song "Bennie and the Jets" was my hit record that I sang for every blue chest appearance. I didn't understand what I was singing and I still don't to this day, but I just love that song. I love Elton John. My favorite album of his is *Goodbye Yellow Brick Road*. He was colorful, wore big glasses, played piano and sang. I wanted to be like him and Stevie Wonder. I was such an odd little girl. I would dance like my mother and pretend I was getting a standing ovation at the end of the song. We lived on that blue chest. My mother's shades gave us a window to a world that only my sister and I would visit to escape the reality of our crazy urban life.

We created a world of our own.

Every great dream begins with a dreamer. Always remember, you have within you

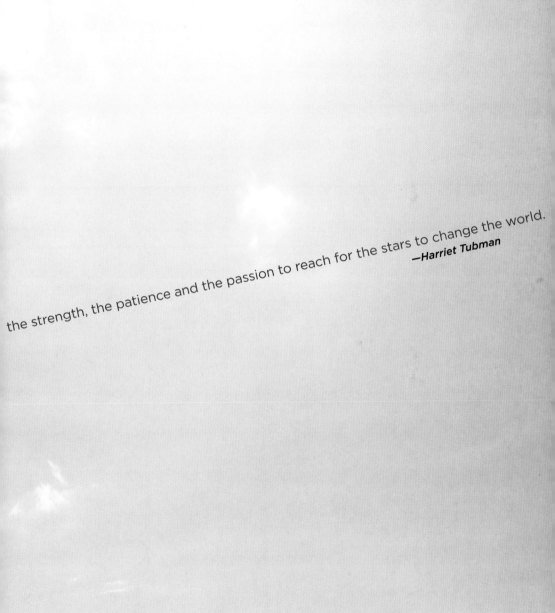

the strength, the patience and the passion to reach for the stars to change the world.

—*Harriet Tubman*

The Gift

I know I complained and took it for granted at times
I know I begged to be rid of this Gift of mine
The power that it has is overwhelming at times for a human being like me
You made me different, but they wanted me to be
A visual for those to see
In a box like the others
Talk bad about my brothers
Wear clear rocks, Bling! Bling!
Like a monkey
Do anything
They wanted me thin with big breasts and fake hair
They wanted me clothed in dental floss, tight jeans and underwear
Stressed out from the pressure to get ahead
I saw Me without the voice
Without vibrations
Without The Gift
I was lost and forced to be still
Just thinking about not singing made me more ill
It made me humble again
The Gift became my friend
And I prayed every day for forgiveness
And cried every night not to feel this
Loss
And you touched me
I felt your love
When the Dr. saw the change
I gave him a hug
And I cried tears of release
And I let go of all that would keep
Me from following my path
From sharing The Gift
Please never, never take it away

I wrote this poem when I lost my voice.

TELL ME I CAN'T SO I CAN SHOW YOU I CAN

My First Time at the Grammys

The red carpet was chaotic and jeweled. A long mile of people wearing designer clothing and lavish jewels hoping to be the fairest or the handsomest of them all. Microphones and flashing lights became attached to their bodies everywhere they walked. A montage of a fashion runway and people running around. It was beautiful and scary all at the same time. Reporter after reporter would ask me, "So how does it feel being nominated for Best New Artist with artists like Amy Winehouse, Taylor Swift and Paramore?" My answer would be the same: "I am honored and I feel like after all this hard work, I am being acknowledged by my peers. I'm honored and I am blessed."

Being bold
and fearless
keeps me one
step ahead.

Between the Lines and Spaces

There is always something in between the lines and spaces of life.

A series of moments where you are figuring things out.

The lines are definite and clear.

There is nothing uncertain when it's on a line.

It's time to win or lose, forgive or stay mad, be sharp or be flat.

In the spaces, we are open to life and open to listen.

We see with our eyes wide open.

Moving with our whole heart and nothing else.

Completely uninhibited and free, ready to experience what life has to offer.

Nothing is for certain, but everything is possible.

I feel that I sing my life.

Now I am writing about my life around the lines and spaces of music.

Going through the minuets of life between the lines and spaces.

hey, you...

Everyone holds their own light.
Always let your light shine.
It doesn't matter if it's not as bright as
   someone else's.
Just keep shining.

I'm a shining star because...

_____

_____

_____

_____

_____

_____

I'm a brand-new me because...

_____

_____

_____

_____

_____

_____

How will I keep on shining?

CHAPTER 5

AUTHENTIC

My shoes
are not your shoes.
These are
my shoes

When you are tempted to give
up, your breakthrough is probably
just around the corner.
—*Joyce Meyer*

Turn
me
loose

When my second major-label release, *Turn Me Loose*, hit the shelves, everyone assumed they knew Ledisi. They called me "The Alright Girl" because of my first single from *Lost and Found*. Yeah, that was me, along with all the albums I've created. But this was a side of me not everyone wanted to hear. When *Turn Me Loose* came out, I was ridiculed more than ever. It was when I premiered my now famous lochawk hairstyle and showed more leg in my photos. The music was louder and in your face, and I gained a diverse and younger audience. I also received two more Grammy nominations. No matter what, some people continued to want Ledisi from the past—jazzy and quiet.

I grew up listening to Willie Nelson, Patsy Cline, The Beatles and Elton John. I love Luther Vandross, Michael Jackson and Anita Baker, but Prince, Fishbone, Lenny Kravitz, U2 and Jimi Hendrix gave me life! Growing up, I had Asian, White, Latino and Black friends. Not all of them listened to R&B, so they introduced me to all kinds of music. During the time I was making *TML*, my friend Cee introduced me to Buddy Miles and I was also hanging out with Mr. Prince. Spending time with him made me go back to listening to music differently. My appreciation for blues/rock guitar came back. He inspired me to stretch out musically and focus on my imagery. I gave the album its title because I didn't want to be boxed in to one version of me. I am limitless when it comes to creating music. I learned that from the greats. The true essence of being authentic is being you. Therefore...I AM.

I am limitless when it comes to creating music. I learned that from the greats.

The Mirrors

When I see myself, I am always looking at my big, round eyes, my
chubby cheeks, my full lips, curvy hips, the annoying pouch called my
tummy, my pointy nose and my long, flowing natural hair...but I never
look into my soul. I avoid it because it requires so much
attention. How is it that I can see all these things and I can't take
the time to look deep into The Mirrors?

"Why?" I ask myself. "Why do you run?"
I let a small sigh escape my lips.
Slowly, I took a deep breath and exhaled.
It's time to allow myself to feel this moment.
What comes to me almost draws me immediately to tears.
I run...because I am still hurting, yearning and, most importantly,
I am still healing. Mama did what she could, but Daddy was not there to teach me. I
guess...running with the wolves has helped me to avoid what is
happening to me now. And now the happening has begun...forcing me to see...
to look in The Mirrors.

Yes, the outside is easy to transform, but the inside has so much hidden.
The bottom of my stomach feels like I ate needles when I think about it.
I'm not ready for this...another sigh escapes me.
Why do I run? Hmmm...I run because I want Love...I want Daddy's Love.
My need for it has grown. I thirst for it, but he does not see me.
I take another look at myself...I see his eyes.
Why was he not there to teach me? Now I look for it...My Man, My Mate...another
mirror. Is he taking Daddy's place? Another sigh comes through me.
Is he the reflection of Daddy? Or is he the daddy I had hoped to see?
The daddy I want to love me and help me be the woman I am hoping to
become. A woman unafraid to look at her soul in The Mirrors.

All these people...all these mirrors around me, I sigh again.
Okay, it's time. Finally, I am going to accept and embrace my reflection
in The Mirrors.

I have to tell myself
I'm beautiful every
day...because every
day the world says
something different.

Yemaya Orisha of the Ocean for Mama

If I had a chance to come back to this life
And make the decision to be who or what
I would like to be you, Mama
I would like to be the ocean
It embraces all that is living
And re-creates all that has died
All the roundness of the earth
It folds, shapes and molds the shores
The depth and its history
Has helped man cross barriers
Enriched, changed, taken and created lives
And above all, it is an essential part of our existence as human beings
It caresses, bathes and nurtures
Our bodies and captures our souls
Without it, we cannot live
The ocean lives in us
Inside we are blue
One color
All her shades of blue complementing the earth
She holds the reflection of the moon
That is the time
We breathe, we grow, we love
Thank you, Mother Ocean
Thank you, Yemaya

Your Existence

Be still from the river of deception that aims to drown you
Fight it hard and be a leader
Demand your existence from those who try to steal it
You are leasing your soul from God until he decides to take it away
Take care of it, guard it, feed it, seize every moment it is filled with, every emotion
that breathes life into every experience we feel as human beings
Triumph over every heartache your soul endures
Use it to heal others
Share the wealth of your wonderful existence

hey, you...

You can't be who they want you to be.
Do you. You are one of a kind.
Be glad in it.
Celebrate your uniqueness.

I don't try
to stand out...
I just do.

Normal is in
the eye of the
beholder.
—Whoopi Goldberg

Miles

There will only be one Miles, a rare gem with bursts of colors. Through sound, vibrant visuals and a natural rebellion against structure, he created a lane of his own. A legacy inspiring an endless generation of beings like me. Miles is my muse, my example of Black pride, and he was unapologetic about the way he expressed himself through his artistry. He orchestrated simplicity, complexity and electricity so brilliantly together. He was one of the reasons I fell in love with jazz. I am excited about life every time I experience him. Thank God for Miles Davis. Thank you for being you. All Shades...All Blues.

How can I be my true self?

_____

_____

_____

_____

_____

_____

_____

Five ways that I'm authentic...

_____

_____

_____

_____

_____

_____

My favorite "keep it real" people are...

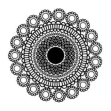

CHAPTER 6

BELIEVE

My Tears Fall...
when a child is born
when everyone sings a song I wrote
when I believe in something
when a new morning comes
when my skin has been satisfied but my heart is still
yearning for the truest form of love
when I do my best and someone less talented gets in front of me
when I've watched *The Color Purple* for the zillionth time
when words say exactly how I feel
when I wake up crying and by the end of the day I manage to smile
when my enemy has become one of my dearest friends
when nothing else matters other than where I am
when someone I love dies
when I hear the words *I LOVE YOU*

Singing in the Bay Area, at times, I felt as if I were a big fish trying to swim in a little pond. Not a good fit. I didn't feel like I had room to grow. I was becoming tired of being a local act, occasionally opening for all the national artists who came to town. I was grateful, but after a while I wanted more. I wanted to grow in a bigger way. I knew my path was leading me to do the hardest thing I had ever done in my life, and that was to leave my comfort zone. I hated the thought of leaving my friends, my house and my family. I loved living in East Oakland and riding down the coast in my car whenever I wanted to get away. But the road was leading me nowhere, just one big circle. I remember one New Year's Eve—after bringing in the New Year riding around the Bay Area with a friend—we thought, *Wow! This is it. This is all we have to look forward to in the future. The same sh#%.* [*Laughing*] I knew

Leaping out
on faith

then that it was time for me to move on. The first step was to quit my job of 12 years. The second step was leaving my band. Each time something pushed me into making a move. It was like God was hearing my heart and helping me out along the way a little bit at a time. Every step required faith. Fame without faith is really a circle of nothing, a circle of the same thing. I knew that if I wanted to be respected and received on a national level, I needed to get out there and do more. I needed to take a leap of faith. I left everything behind. Only a few people supported me. I learned that not everyone believes in your dream as much as you believe in it. I think the most hurtful lesson for me during the process of elevating my career was learning that the people closest to you are the ones who can hurt you the most. It took me many years after I left Oakland to figure that out. But I wouldn't change a thing. I was finally headed in a path of the unknown, and if I wanted to grow, this was the right thing for me to do. I auditioned for a role as an understudy in the Broadway musical *Caroline or Change*. It was about change, and I was changing. Taking that job changed my life. I had decided it was time to throw caution to the wind and move to New York City.

Although it's
hard, you have
to move in
order to grow.

You just can't sit there and wait for people to give you the golden dream. You've got to go out there and make it happen for yourself.
—*Diana Ross*

YOU MUST BELIEVE BEFORE OTHERS BELIEVE

To capture the moment is to live in the moment.

What I believe is...

_____

_____

_____

_____

_____

_____

What gives me faith is...

_____

_____

_____

_____

_____

_____

_____

_____

I leapt out on faith when...

_____

_____

_____

_____

_____

_____

_____

_____

_____

_____

_____

_____

_____

_____

_____

_____

_____

_____

CHAPTER 7

FORGIVENESS

Forgive your enemies,
but never forget their names.
—*John F. Kennedy*

thought I was having a nightmare and if I woke up it would end. But as I became a bit clearer about my surroundings, I realized I had been abruptly awakened and was entering a nightmare. The colors went from a sleepy orange and I felt myself falling through this blue tunnel. Everything was blue and then my mind, body and soul were alive and my eyes were open. My stepfather touched me and the little girl became Blue. No more orange, no more sunshine, no more peppermint sticks and Sour Apple Now and Laters while jumping rope. Superman became the devil and God was nowhere to be found. I asked God, "Why me? Why is this happening to me?" There was no answer, just the smell of stained beer on a smelly robe invading the air in the room. I couldn't breathe. I couldn't move. Why am I frozen? I looked up

Little girl Blue

at the ceiling of my room that was no longer my haven. It was a cage and I could no longer fly. This was where I flew, daydreaming about singing on big stages, music playing on my General Electric radio elevating my spirit. Now it was a cage where the little girl became Blue. He touched me more, hands shaking because the sin was alive and the devil lived. The same devil taught me about the drums, how to play. "Come on, you can do it," he would say. "You can keep the beat, Cee." That was my nickname: Cee. He would protect me from others, but who was going to protect me from him? Who was going to protect me from the devil? The devil taught me how to fish and how to roller-skate. The same devil taught me how to pray.

Like a movie, my memory played back the moments. The times he would look at me when I washed the dishes and how he just happened to be near the bathroom door after I would take a shower. I finally understood I was being watched through the peephole of the bathroom door and watched as I walked around the safe place I called home. I was being preyed on and I felt the

discomfort but did not pay attention. Suddenly, the tears came. Guilt came. Maybe this was my fault. I should have protected myself better. The final lesson he was now teaching me was how to HATE: "Where are you, God? Are you gonna come and save me? I've been a good girl. I really tried to be good. I go to church every Sunday and practice the piano at the church on Saturdays." The tears fell harder and finally a sound escaped my lips and the touching stopped as if an alarm had gone off. The apologies began, and he moved away from me and quickly left the room: "Please, don't tell anyone." The devil was here and his smell lingered. I lay there in tears until my blue body and my blue spirit fell asleep.

When I woke up, I told Mama, and her face was blank. She didn't go to work that day. She made me go to school. Orange never came back until I left home, when I turned 18. I was in my twenties when the devil called asking for forgiveness. I forgave him so I could live. I remember he would tell me over and over, "You will never be nothing. You're not good enough to be anything." It was the beginning of a long line of rejections, but also the beginning of a long list of triumphs. He tried to kill my spirit from the time I was born, but every day I breathe I beat him. I beat the devil. Every day I win. Every day I stomp him.

Scars

Scars heal, but they leave a mark
Some people pick on it and it never heals, it just keeps bleeding
Even though you have forgiven those who caused the scar,
it is still there, seen or unseen
It still lives
Sometimes...
Sometimes you touch that spot and the memory repeats itself
Some scars are so deep mentally they come back at a certain time,
a particular day, through someone or a place
A scar, a noun leading to the adjective called remembering
Remembering when it hurt

hey, you...

Let it go.
Release all that...it's not worth it.
Move on...get out of your way.
The best part of your life is waiting for you.

There is
nothing
more
complex
than
understanding
yourself.

Love
yourself
again

I know...

...that people cannot read my mind, but I expect them to

...that I am afraid every day of making mistakes, but I walk through my fears every day

...I like being alone, but I make sure I am around people to learn more about myself

...that I cannot fix everything, but I sure try because I care so much about people

...I am still hurting over some things in my past, but I choose to sing about it, write it in a song or say it out loud...that could be a bad thing

...now that most people are not as fearless as me, but I am more fearful than most

...people who judge others for living their dream are scared to fully leap out and live their own

...I have blue words and my fist closed when I see people hurting others, especially children

...I can't forgive people who lie

...that none of us can hide from the truth, no matter how far we try to run from it

JOURNAL ENTRY: People

Heading home from Germany, I had a layover in Africa. At my gate, I sat near the door. I began to write in my journal. Occasionally, I would look up and observe my surroundings, allowing myself to be inspired by all the interesting people at the airport.

A tall, lean gentleman the color of coal sat next to me with his briefcase and smiled. His teeth were white like pearls and his eyes lit up when I looked at him. We both smiled and greeted each other with a simple nod. He spoke first, " My sistah! What part of Africa are you from?" I spoke, " I am not originally from Africa. I am from the United States, but my ancestry originates from Nigeria." His smile went away so quickly you would have thought I called him a bad word. He said nothing after I spoke and quickly moved away. I watched him as he walked away, and he sat four rows away from me. I was so hurt that I put on my shades so no one could see me cry.

I cried all the way home. That man saw me and noticed that I was in tears. I think he felt sorry for what he had done, and he tried several times to get closer and talk to me. He tried to sit next to me on the plane, but someone had taken that seat. When the plane landed in New York, he followed me as I walked to my connecting flight." Excuse me, sistah. My sistah!" he said. He tapped me on my shoulder. I stopped walking and took off my shades and looked at him directly in his eyes. My eyes were red and puffy. He moved in close to me as if to whisper, " Why were you crying?" I answered," You know why I was crying." He touched my hand and said, " Please forgive me." I smiled and said, " I already have." I put my shades on and walked away to catch my connecting flight.

Just like my favorite hero, Muhammad Ali, says:
" It isn't the mountains ahead to climb that wear you out...
it's the pebble in your shoe."
YES!

Forgive yourself for any mistakes you made

Be grateful when a new day comes

It's another day to be a better you

It's
not
my
fault

Path to forgiveness

Dear_____,

Being forced to put my feelings in a letter is torture for me right now. I hope to get through all this. Let me start by saying I am sorry if I ever hurt your feelings. I never meant to hurt you. Please accept my apology. I am sorry for asking for a love you can't give right now. You are still trying to figure out who you are. I know that you care about me and you have given me what you could give. Thank you. I thank you for the journey. This experience has taken me on a wonderful journey of elevating myself spiritually. It is a journey I have always wanted to embrace, and because of us, I have found it. Finally, good things have happened to me. Changes I never thought would exist have manifested and I am blessed. And three of the most incredible things have happened in the process of finding God.

The first thing has been understanding the kind of love I want and deserve. I know that because I have opened up to you. And even though I did not find forever with you, and as painful as it is right now, I wouldn't change a thing. The second is learning to love myself. I am learning to treat myself to the finer things in life. Never putting myself second to anything or anyone. The third thing and best part of it all is finding God and knowing that His love is always there. And it doesn't hurt to LOVE.

I share this with you only because I feel so much joy in this process. The process of forgiveness. At the same time, unfortunately, I am unhappy because I can't bring myself to be your friend right away. You never gave me clarity, respect and honesty, which are the basis of any kind of relationship. Had you been some or all those things, I think we could have embarked on a friendship right away. So, right now, I need this time to keep reminding myself of who I am and ask God to help me forgive you enough to be your friend. I don't mean that to be mean. Nothing in this letter is to lash out. I just wanted to share with you my reasons for not being your friend. I don't expect anything from you. I only hope that you have learned something from our time together.

But that is not for me to say. I have enjoyed our time together and again I thank you for it.

Best of luck.

I forgive you: _____

_____

_____

_____

_____

_____

I forgive me for...

_____

_____

_____

_____

_____

_____

_____

I'll never forget when...

_____

_____

_____

_____

_____

_____

_____

Who do you forgive?

_____

_____

_____

_____

_____

_____

_____

_____

_____

_____

_____

_____

_____

_____

_____

_____

_____

_____

_____

_____

This is a day of new beginnings. I will...

CHAPTER 8

TREASURES

The journey has a beginning and a middle, but
it never ends. That is what living feels like. Life
is like jazz to me. I'm always improvising.
I know the form of the song and the
melody, but somewhere in its structure,
there is freedom to tell the story. That's
the sweetest gift God gave us.
The beauty to venture out

I always find
a connection
with Ms. Nina.

t was on a Sunday I heard a Nina Simone song on the radio. It was playing on a public radio station in the Bay Area and the song was "Trouble in Mind." It was a beautiful day, and I was sitting in my white rocking chair on my porch. The door to my house was wide open as the radio blasted from inside my living room. I didn't care if the entire neighborhood could hear it! I was feeling good about myself because I was a young new home owner. I had heard Nina's music before, because my mama used to play her records and sing "Mississippi Goddam" all

Nina on Sundays

the time when I was a little girl. It was the song she would sing to wake me and my sister up in the mornings for school. We would moan and groan about getting up, but Mama would keep singing the song until we finally got out of bed. I never saw Ms. Nina's face, but I knew her name. I definitely remembered that voice. It always stopped me in my tracks.

Once again, her voice made me still. This time I was on my porch, and I was finally listening to her on my own as an adult. That piano rolled into my ears like a train and she meant it that way. I closed my eyes, sitting alone on my sofa crying after she sang, "But I won't be blue always." My tears and her voice went on and on, and in my soul, it felt so familiar. She was singing about my loneliness and that was the moment I connected with Queen Nina Simone. I never thought that singing her song "Four Women" years later at Black Girls Rock would literally catapult my career to such an unimaginable level. Her legacy lifted me and reminded me to be proud of my skin and embrace the walk I was given. I truly hope I made her proud. Every now and then I think to myself, *I hope she can feel how much I love her.* She has saved my life so many times. Her music lets me know I am not alone in my journey. It's alright to be different. I adore Ms. Nina Simone! I always remember her spirit by listening to her music every Sunday.

Sometimes being a friend means mastering the art of timing. There is a time for silence. A time to let go and allow people to hurl themselves into their own destiny. And a time to prepare to pick up the pieces when it's all over.
—*Octavia Butler*

Left: Me with Roland Jack, my best friend, tour manager and living diary

Real Friends

Real friends won't let you touch the bottom. They catch you before you fall. They tell you when you're wrong and push you until you're right. They support you in whatever you want to do, but if they disagree, they will give you what you don't want to hear.

From left: Troy Saunders and Darryl Hill (RIP); Wanda Tidline; singers Laurnea and Kim Hill and writer Ernest Hardy; PJ Morton; Yvonne and Wanda Tidline; Eric Benet; Fred Hammond; Kenyatte Brown (my best friend for more than 15 years)

They love you hard and will eventually forgive you. They expect nothing other than your best. They already know you feel the same way about them and will do anything for them, because that is what real friends do.

YOU CAN'T LET YOUR FAILURES DEFINE YOU— YOU HAVE TO LET THEM TEACH YOU.

—President Barack Obama

THE GREATEST GIFT IS NOT BEING AFRAID TO QUESTION. —RUBY DEE

hey, you...

Treasure every moment God gives you.
Make memories that last a lifetime.
Create memories that remind you of Love.

Rise Above It All

I've been there too
Uncertain and confused
Searching relentlessly for my source
Found higher power and became a force
It was a voice, I heard it say
A phrase I say today

You must Rise above it all
Get back up if you should fall
Don't look down, walk proud, stand tall
You must Rise above it all

Nonbelievers won't believe
Until what you say is finally seen
And all your dreams, they will come true
Every dream begins with you

Every journey has a lesson
How you listen holds the blessing
So I hope your ears were open
To the words that I have spoken
I will say it once again
Because I care and I'm your friend
You will need this phrase one day
Please remember what I say

You must Rise above it all
Get back up if you should fall
Don't look down, walk proud, stand tall
You must Rise above it all

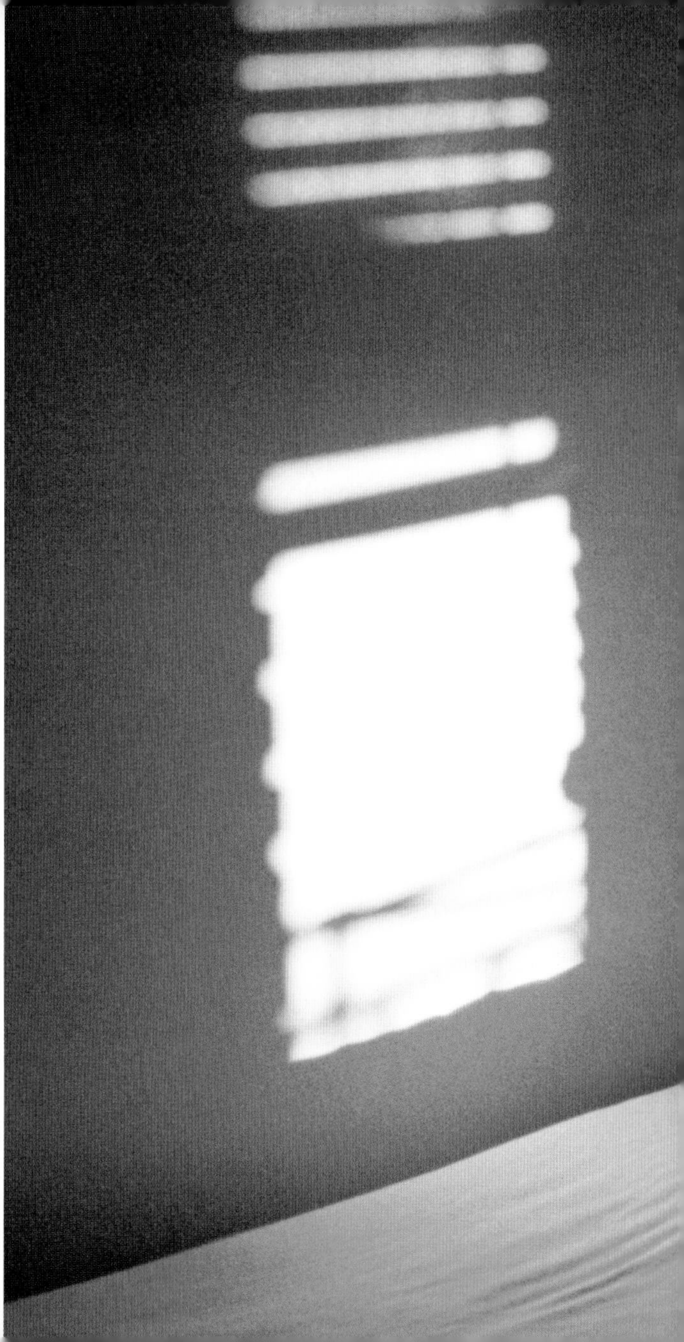

JOURNAL ENTRY: Talking to the Floor

I slept in a sleeping bag next to Richard's bed every night, and every night I felt horrible. I was miserable, but at least I wasn't out on the street or spending all my money on a hotel. I was lucky I had a place to sleep. The floor represented failure for me. I was ashamed, and I didn't tell anyone about it. One night I really started talking to myself on the floor. When I think about it, I was really talking to God. I started thinking about all the reasons I had gotten here. I thought about the people I had in my life and how they helped me grow. And all the opportunities I missed because I listened to those same people who were nowhere to be found when I needed them. I was mad at myself for allowing so much in and not protecting myself better and knowing my value. I thought about how insecure I was and that I didn't love myself enough to think that I deserved the best. The people who said they love me should be here for me right now and where are they? And that's when I changed my thinking. Wait a minute. God has been clearing the way for me because I couldn't do it for myself. All I needed and wanted was coming to me once I looked at my mistakes and learned from them. HE has never left me. I needed to see that HE will never let me down. I started to see that I was ungrateful for all the beautiful experiences God had given me thus far. I didn't enjoy what I had been given, nor did I thank God for all the places HE took me. I just kept asking for more. I cried and prayed that night. I was grateful to my friend Richard for helping me get to New York. I decided to never forget this night. I took responsibility for all the decisions I had made. I had no one else to blame but myself for being right here. Talking to the floor...talking to God.

"I believe in human beings, and that all human beings should be respected as such, regardless of their color."

—Malcolm X

Malcolm X,
a class act

Concrete jungle

New York City was loud and noisy, and already I was getting a headache and doubting if I had made the right decision moving here. I was so used to my rocking chair on my porch and the peaceful sounds of the birds tweeting in the big tree in my backyard. Instead, I was pulling two big suitcases up a flight of stairs to my friend Richard's apartment. Feeling overwhelmed with the time change, I almost didn't have it in me to tell Richard how excited I was about my future.

The next day I was in a cab headed to a fitting for my costumes for the show, and my phone rang. "Lady C?" a deep old man's voice said on the phone. I answered, "Hello? Ifa! No, this is not my mom. Who is this?" "Lady C, this is your father, Larry Sanders." The cab driver honked his horn and yelled, "Move out of the way, asshole!" It scared me and I almost dropped the phone. I was silent. I grew up not knowing about my real father. My stepfather was a talented drummer, but selfish, abusive and evil. He was my only introduction to what a father was. Here I was, my second day in New York City, on the phone with my real father. Before I left Oakland, I found him and sent a letter along with my two independent albums, asking him to reach out when he could.

My friends introduced me to his music when I was visiting Amsterdam. I tracked Daddy down through his lawyer, but I never thought he would call. "Hello?" his voice sounded gentle yet concerned. I said, "Yes, this is me, Ledisi." He laughed and said, "I've missed you so much. I love you and I have so much to say to you." I looked at the phone and the number was blocked. I explained that it was hard to hear him but I hoped we could talk again. He said, "I'm going to call you again. I promise. I have some things I must do first now that I am certain this is you. I'll call you tomorrow." I said, "I would love that."

He went on the explain more things, but I can't remember everything because I was in shock. When we hung up I sat in the car near tears trying to figure out how to process our conversation. I couldn't believe I had finally spoken to my real father after all these years. What do I do with all this? I made

I couldn't believe I had finally spoken to my real father after all these years.

it to my fitting and received my music for rehearsals, moving in a daze and wondering when would be a good time to call my mother. So much to tell her in one day.

When I was done with rehearsal and meeting my new cast, I walked about 18 New York blocks back to the apartment (carrying a big binder of the script and music in my backpack) and thought about my life and allowed myself to embrace my new home. The hot smell of wasted food, fresh grilled chicken from the corner trucks and gasoline invaded my senses. The loud music from open bars and laughter from people talking about their day evoked more adventure. But when I stopped to look at some of the store windows with elegant gowns, I began to face my reality. I was unable to afford anything, not even a slice of pizza, after selling so many albums. I had $68 in my bank account and a mortgage for a house I didn't live in. I started crying, *How did I get here?* I walked more and hoped no one could see my tears. *Lord, I don't know where I am headed, but I promise I'm going to make the best of it.*

A new day

OR MY GREAT EXPERIENCE WITH CHAKA KHAN

It had almost been a year since I was last onstage and I was slowly doing everything I could to fade away. It was almost working until God changed the plan. The only thing that pulled me back was a phone call from my booking agent telling me that Chaka Khan wanted me to do a week of shows with her as the opening act. I could not believe it! I immediately called my mom to ask her what to do. She screamed at me, "You gotta do it. She asked for you!" The thing that made me uncomfortable was the prospect of playing with my old band again. Not because I didn't like their playing but because of the tension between us since I had moved to New York. Just the thought of playing with them again made my stomach turn. I was not happy about going back, but I couldn't share this moment with any other group of musicians. They helped me get to where I was. The first scheduled show was at The Saratoga Mountain Winery, an outdoor concert venue where the fireflies lit up the night and you could see the sunset and drink wine while you watched a show. Such a beautiful place to see Chaka Khan sing all her hits. It was my first Chaka Khan concert and I had the wonderful opportunity to open for her. Ironically, this was the same place I saw my first concert ever, featuring George Benson and Dianne Reeves. So this venue held great memories for me.

I was trying my best to shake the awkwardness of performing with my old band again, because some of the members were pretty mean. I really wanted to leave but decided to hold my peace. [*Laughing*] Regardless of how I felt, I was not gonna let my differences with some band members ruin my experience of opening for Chaka Khan. It was the only reason I decided to get back onstage again. I invited my mom to the show to be my place of solace. She

Bold and beautiful

was so excited. When I was little, Mom would play Chaka's music around the house and she sang Chaka Khan and Rufus songs with her band. I never knew the words, but I knew Chaka's voice and I knew the melodies. The energy in the crowd was electric—it felt like all of Oakland had attended this event to witness Ledisi and Chaka Khan on the same bill together. It truly was a magical night. I was extremely nervous, and I hoped my set had made a great impression. To tell you the truth, I didn't remember anything about my part of the show. That was how it always was performing with my old band. I never remembered how things went; I was just happy to get through it. The audience did seem to have loved the show. I changed my clothes and pulled my mother along to sit next to me while we waited for Chaka to come onstage. We purposely sat far in the back, hoping no one would see us. We were so excited that we could just watch the show like everyone else. Just Mom and me at the Chaka Khan concert. The lights went down and the guitar began to wail as the drums pounded out the beats. In a beautiful rock star outfit, Chaka came onstage to a fan blowing her hair back. Looking sultry and instantly dominating the audience. She was here. She hit notes that made me cry. Her band played hard and her singers were mimicking every note she hit. My mom and I were screaming as we watched Chaka glide through notes, putting all of us in a frenzy. The sky was filled with fireflies, and people stayed on their feet. Halfway into her set, she was about to perform a Marvin Gaye classic, "What's Going On." He is one of my all-time favorite male vocalists. I loved her even more because she loved him as well. She asked, "Where is Ledisi?" My mouth flew open and I looked at my mom as the audience screamed. I asked her, "Did she say my name?" She said, "Yes! She said your name twice, and she wants you to go onstage and sing with her." I just sat there in disbelief as people started pointing toward me and my mom. I couldn't move. So I started shaking my head no. Mom started laughing and pushed me, "Girl, get up!" I stood up and the crowd got louder. I was so embarrassed because I had on shorts, a T-shirt and a head wrap. I had not planned to go on-stage with her. I looked a hot mess. [*Laughing*] I made it to the stage shaking and near tears. Chaka hugged me and asked me to sing the song with her. She was even more beautiful up close. Then I started to panic because I never know the words to other artists' songs. I know melodies, but I never memorize all the words, just some of them. It was too late. I was onstage with the great Chaka Khan. I can't remember much after the song started. When I got offstage, I made my way back to my mother, who was crying her eyes out. Chaka Khan and Nancy Wilson are her favorite female vocalists, so I was living her dream. I asked my mom, "How did I do?" She told me it was awesome and that Chaka had helped me with some of the words. I squeezed my mom really tight and said, "Mom, can you believe it? I met Chaka Khan!" That week with Chaka was the last time I performed with my old band and that week also made me want to start performing again. If it weren't for Chaka Khan giving me that opportunity to share the stage with her, I think my story would have had a different outcome.

> *I asked her, "Did Chaka say my name?" Mom said, "Yes! she said your name twice, and she wants you to go onstage to sing with her."*

Don't tell me
dreams don't
come true.

CHAPTER 9

ALRIGHT

I
beat
the
devil.
Every
day
I
win

Writing
"Alright"

Sleeping on the floor in a New York City apartment, in a small bedroom next to a friend's bed, was a blessing for me. I was grateful I had a place to sleep. At least that's what I told myself every night in the midst of my tears. I couldn't believe my life had come to this. After all that hard work releasing two successful albums independently and doing theater for 12 years, I was here on the floor, in a sleeping bag. It was my small piece of the world. I was so depressed, even though I had a job on Broadway as an understudy. My friend Richard had introduced me to the world of theater, New York–style, and it saved my life. But my heart was still empty. I found a new life on Broadway and it had embraced me, but my old life as a recording artist began to resurface. Every day, people would ask me when I was going to sing again. Labels were beginning to look for me again. I was too embarrassed to tell them I had given up. I was comfortable hiding on Broadway. I was insecure with a hole in my soul. I yearned to be onstage singing but was mad at all the pain being an artist had caused me, so I kept refusing.

The moment that pushed me to my end was when I opened for Aretha Franklin at the Hammerstein Ballroom. I wanted so badly to have the right band and sing the right songs to impress The Queen and her court. However, instead of the moment adjusting to me, I had to adjust to the moment once again. The promoters allowed me to work with only a piano player they provided. I found this out after I had agreed to do the show. To add insult to injury, I wasn't getting paid. I smiled through it and performed the way I knew how, singing songs I didn't want to sing. The audience loved it, but I felt used. It was not the moment I wanted. I watched Ms. Franklin sing her hits, wishing I could have had a chance to talk to her and ask her how to deal with the ups and downs. People told me I was awesome, but my heart was broken. One record executive I knew whispered to me that night, "You should stop singing R&B and just become a jazz singer." I think I cried all night, and when the sun came up I had made my decision: I was just going to teach and quit the business.

I called my mom and told her, "I can't do this anymore, so I'm leaving this business. I'm always being told I am not pretty enough, I'm too jazzy, I'm not a star. I'm tired of being broke. I did my best. I'll bow out and teach someone else to be great." She said, "I don't want to hear all that. You're going through things, Ledisi, but you're going to be alright." I thought to myself, *Wow, that sounds like a song!* I talked to my mom some more and then I called my boyfriend. He talked to me almost all the way home to Oakland. I had a flight to catch and he would not hang up the phone. He was on the East Coast and I tried to give him many reasons why I could no longer be in this business. He told me every reason why I should be in the business and how much I was needed. He was doing his best to persuade me not to quit. He called when I landed and talked to me until I made it home. He was not giving up on me and made me promise him I would never stop singing.

I remember going into a recording session with producer Rex Rideout, explaining to him about my journey as an artist. He went in on me as well. So I had to promise my mother, my boyfriend and Rex to never give up. All these conversations inspired the song "Alright." It became the first single from my Grammy-nominated album *Lost & Found*. That CD brought me my first two Grammy nominations, one of them as Best New Artist. I'm so glad they never let me give up.

Alright

This life can make me so confused, but it's alright
Living day by day I feel so used, and that ain't right
I just want to run and hide, but I don't have the time to cry
And it's alright, it's alright
Many thoughts are running through my head, it's alright
Wishing to be somewhere else but here, and it's alright
I can't wait to see your face, I need a smile and your embrace
And I'm alright, I'm alright

Life can bring us through many changes, it's alright
Just don't give up, know that it's gonna be alright
People come and they go, that's just the way that it goes, it's alright

Sometimes the rain it makes me sad, but it's alright
Some things in the world, they make me mad, and it's alright
In the morning when I see the sun, I know I'm not the only one
And I'm alright, I'm alright...hey
I wish I had some money to pay my bills
I can't even buy that dress on sale, but it's alright
Having money don't mean a thing, but loving you is everything
And I'm alright, I'm alright...yeah

Life can bring us through many changes, it's alright
Just don't give up, know that it's gonna be alright
People come and they go, that's just the way that it goes, it's alright

Whoa...everything is everything
Whoa...it's gonna be alright
Whoa...everything is everything
Whoa...it's gonna be alright

Life can bring us through many changes, it's alright
Just don't give up, know that it's gonna be alright
People come and they go, that's just the way that it goes, it's alright

hey, you...

You can read books about life,
but there is nothing greater than
experiencing it for yourself.

I'm alright because...

_____

_____

_____

_____

_____

_____

_____

One day I'm going to...

_____

_____

_____

_____

_____

_____

_____

_____

_____

_____

Who makes me feel better than alright?

_____

_____

_____

_____

_____

_____

_____

_____

_____

_____

_____

_____

_____

_____

_____

_____

_____

_____

_____

_____

_____

CHAPTER 10

HOME

Once you plant the
seed, it will grow

Grandma
Lorraine

I remember her hands and her tight pencil skirt and her high-heel shoes. I was too little to remember all the details of her face, but I loved her red lipstick. She was a hot Brown Betty. She was very beautiful to me. Grandma Lorraine had a shape like Dorothy Dandridge, but was very conservative in the way she carried herself. Still, she wore tailored clothing that showed off her figure. In the kitchen, she was not a great cook, but she tried and demanded you eat her food. She didn't play either. The stuffed pepper given to me one night at dinner towered on my plate like a giant green meatball. "You betta eat all your food," she said.

Afraid to speak, I looked over to my mom because Grandma Lorraine had a voice like a teacher. Later, I found out she was a chemistry and biology professor at a college in a rural part of Louisiana called Winnfield.

She later moved to New York. All I really knew about her was her passion for books and education and that the men loved her. She passed those traits on to my mom, who passed them on to us. [*Laughing*] I'm referring to the education part in particular. [*Laughing*] The men always complimented her on her legs.

My sister Tamyra looks the most like her. Mom told me about how she loved to go dancing, hang out with her girlfriends and hear live music. Grandma Lorraine was brilliant and knew how to carry herself. She was very fashionable and always a lady. I love the old pictures of her. She was just so beautiful and stylish. I love you, Grandma Lorraine! Whenever I wear my red pumps and my red lipstick, I do it in tribute to you.

This poem "Forgive Me" was inspired when I was traveling on the airplane looking out the window. I was on my way to my grandmother's funeral. This is what I felt she would have wanted to say to all those who mourned her.

I read this at her funeral.

I love the old pictures of her. She was just so beautiful and stylish. I love you, Grandma Lorraine!

Forgive Me

Forgive me
For not loving you like I wanted to
Forgive me
For not giving you more of what you
   deserved
For showing you more strength and a
   little less love
Forgive me, for I tried to do my best
Please forgive me for not telling you
   how beautiful you turned out to be
For not saying I love you
Please know that I do
Forgive me
My daughter, my son
My nieces, my nephews
My friends, forgive me
Because I forgive you
Because I love you
We celebrate her life and
   the beginning of her new life with God
We love you, Grandma Lo
A part of me for Grandma Lo
I saw the moon dance on the water
And it smiled at me
I saw the waves curve around its light
And that moved me
I almost touched heaven
But a star was in my way.
And I soared on the airplane like a
   metal bird
It was the closest I could get to you
I felt tears come to my eyes
Because I realized you were too far
   away for me to touch
But a smile came back to my face
You will always be a part of my life

From top: Great-
Aunt ReGusta; my
greatgrandparents'
family church;
Grandma Lorraine

Jessi

Learn to value the people who value you.

—*Bill Withers*

Thank you for who you are
thank you for being my shining star
thank you for the role model I need to see
thank you for showing how much you love me
for all the things you've done and said
Even for smacking me in my big head 😊
Not only are you my sister but also my friend
thank you for sticking with me from the
thick to the thin . . . .

1/17/00 *mf*

Mama in the 9th grade

From left:
Me at 6
years old;
Mama at 14
being fast

Above right:
Mama at 17 years
old. Left: Mama
and I backstage
in Oakland

Aunt Gussie

SHE TAUGHT MY MAMA AND ME HOW TO SING

Great-Aunt
ReGusta
McDaniel

She was and still is my favorite aunt, my great-aunt ReGusta McDaniel. We called her "Gu" or "Gussie." I loved going to her house because she always had sweets in the kitchen and cherry tomatoes in the backyard. She was always dressed, even if it was to go outside to the mailbox. She was beautiful, even in her tennis shoes. She was very strict, but loved us all as if she had given birth to my mom and my sisters and me. She spoke clearly and always held her head up high. When she smiled, it was like Christmas, and she gave so much to those she loved. I loved her spirit, but like the rest of the people in our world we loved her voice. It sounded like heaven. Her voice was reminiscent of Leontyne Price and Mahalia Jackson with the presence of Louis Armstrong. She made you happy and feel good when you watched her sing, but her voice was so BIG. She never needed a mic, just a handkerchief and a song. If she called your name, her voice felt like it made the house shake. She never gave us spankings, she would just yell and we would break out into tears. She was all bark and cupcakes inside. Everyone says I look and sound like her. I always think about her when I sing gospel music.

Gu only sang in church, taking pride in singing for the Lord. She was a favorite soloist at the neighborhood

Baptist church. Her most popular requested song was "Thy Grace Is Sufficient for Me." The church was always hot and everyone had picture-paper church fans. You know, the kind with the wooden stick stapled at the end to create a handle. Gu would be at the top of the choir stand waiting for the pianist to play her introduction. Poised and upright, she moved slowly in her stacked-high heels and perfectly pressed Sunday dress, with her pearls and a flower pinned like a badge of honor on her shoulder. She gracefully took her place to sing for the Saints. With a beautiful handkerchief in her right hand and no microphone, she began with one note that would soar through the hot air like a cool breeze, demanding the attention of all those attending the service.

Immediately, the people would start shouting. I remember Gu walking down the choir stand slowly, blessing the room with high and low notes, ending each phrase with a smile. She would eventually make her way into the congregation and people would start jumping and shouting, "Gloray!" She never broke her presence in the spirit of the song, and by the time the song was ending, she was back at the top of the choir stand where she began. Not a hair out of place, not one slight smudge of sweat on her makeup and her handkerchief was still fresh and clean. While she sat poised, the congregation was in a flurry and the organist played a reprise. Folks were passing out and jumping up and down calling out, "Jesus!" Seeing all the tears streaming down their faces, I would hold close to my mother, not fully understanding what was happening. I just knew it was alright because Gussie sat in the choir stand smiling.

She never broke her presence in the spirit of the song...she was back at the top of the choir stand.

Katrina

I FELT SO HELPLESS

We're leaving. I don't think we can stay. It's not looking good, so we're going to head out to Dallas." My older sister had so much fear in her voice as she spoke to me. I didn't want her to hang up. "Well, what are you taking with you?" I asked, trying not to sound worried. "As much stuff as we can, mainly our pictures. I'll call you when we get to Texas," she said.

I hated to hang up. I wished there were something I could do. I felt so helpless. I think I bit off all my nails thinking about them traveling to get to Dallas. We watched the news, and mom told me some of our family members couldn't afford to leave. They had been through many hurricanes, but this one was different. The newscasters said it was one of the biggest hurricanes since the 1800's. My little family on Fig Street had survived them all. I was praying they would get through this one as well. I thought about my friends and wondered about their families. I called everyone I knew and asked them how they were getting out. In my adult years, I found myself visiting New Orleans so much that I began thinking of finding a place down there. We had just buried my great-aunt Gussie. The heaviest burden was on my sister Shannon, who had lived in New Orleans all her life and raised her children there. This was the hurricane that forced them to leave.

The months became years after Katrina, and I watched my sister's life turn upside down. I sent what I could and had people send things to my family.

St. Louis in the French Quarter

Great-Aunt Virginia

All of it helped, but it never stopped her from longing to be home. She has not been the same since Katrina. I was thrilled they were alright and safe, but when I followed her journey through Katrina and the aftermath of it, I was so sad and upset by all the things they went through just to get their lives back on track. Other family members had died and some suffered for days without food and water. They endured rape and beatings. Later, they prayed for trailer homes so they could stay in New Orleans. Things got better for my family as a whole, but their spirits haven't been the same since Katrina. Even though things are looking up, it still hasn't cured the heartbreak in the spirit of the people in New Orleans. The BP Gulf oil spill disaster a little less than five years later hasn't helped matters. Nonetheless, we made it through. What I love about New Orleans is that we never give up, and I am honored to have roots in a place with such resilient, proud people. It will always be a place I call home. Recently, I lost the last of my great-aunts, Aunt Virginia. She was a powerful leader in the New Orleans community and more than 400 people attended her funeral. I could not be there because my mother was ill at the time of the services. All my great-aunts have passed away, but I still have family in New Orleans holding on to their land and strengthening their family bond. My sister has finally moved back and is slowly rebuilding her life in New Orleans again. I am proud of her, and I'm planning on investing in property there as well. That will ensure that I will always have a home in New Orleans.

hey, you...

Find a place of peace.
Stay there and reflect on your life.
It could have been better or worse.
But guess what? You made it!
You are living and breathing
And you get another chance to add
    more good to your life.

It's not about you...
it's about what God
is going to do in your life.
—T.D. Jakes

A Memphis
tree

NEVER FORGET THOSE WHO CAME BEFORE YOU. ALWAYS REMEMBER YOUR ROOTS!

Reflections

I wrote the song "Sweet Magnolia" with Xavier Mosley, aka Chief Xcel, who is one of my best friends. We formed a group called Loudspeaker, which is the fusion of hip-hop and R&B. Our music centers around social issues as well as love and elevating conscious thinking. The magnolia is the official state flower of Louisiana, and I wanted to write a song depicting our anger at how New Orleans was handled during the aftermath of Hurricane Katrina. We watched it on television, and I can't begin to express how upset I was that no one was doing anything but watching people suffer. It was heartbreaking.

Sweet Magnolia

This house filled with water so deep
Goes much deeper than the sea
Filled with spirits here before me
Did you see me on the TV?
Did you cry watching all people die?
Still nobody answered why
Why did all the time go by
  waiting for someone to save me?
Sweet Magnolia
Sweet Magnolia
So sweet
Sweet Magnolia
So Sweet...So Sweet
Be still
How can peace be still
  when there is a void to fill?
Quick to holla "let's rebuild"
What about the soulless bodies?
My heart, Mother Nature broke my heart
Exposing what was in the dark
How do I begin to start?

Did you see me on the TV?
Sweet Magnolia
Sweet Magnolia
So sweet
Sweet Magnolia
So Sweet...So Sweet
Misplaced
Nowhere really can replace
History I can't erase
Tears keep fallin' down my face
Did you see me on the TV?
My home
Everything I had is gone
Leaving me to feel alone
I hope this don't last too long
Did someone really save me?

Sweet Magnolia
Sweet Magnolia
So sweet
Sweet Magnolia
So Sweet...So Sweet

Elders I cherish...

_____

_____

_____

_____

_____

_____

_____

My next family gathering is...

_____

_____

_____

_____

_____

_____

_____

Family Photos

(Place your visuals here)

CHAPTER 11

TAKE A BOW

It's going to
be alright!

W hen you expect the best, the best will come—but sometimes not in the manner or time frame you want it. In life, we are taught to be patient. Understanding patience does not come easily. I know because I have patience the size of a pea. I am horrible at waiting and I want things now. So I am sure you can guess that I am constantly working on myself. [*Laughing*] "The best is yet to come"...that phrase drives me batty. When? That is always my first question. The second is, Why not now? In true Ledisi fashion, my childlike spirit is wanting to know the answers right away. As life would have it, my journey is about expecting the unexpected. I say it to others every day, but I am also saying it to myself.

You can expect the best, but the best will come at an undisclosed time. That is how life is. The best does not come when you want it. It comes when it is time. There is always a lesson you must learn. You might already learn the lesson and what you expect comes right away. Sometimes it comes when everything is in alignment. All you can control is how you deal with the journey. What you invest in your journey will add to the success of your expectation. Your sacrifices, your belief system, being humble and being brave to do things differently all add to your success. These are life's lessons. What is meant for you is simply meant for you. You cannot compare yourself to others. Your journey is completely different. You are similar in that you exist to do what you are doing at that moment and no one else can do it like you.

Expect the unexpected

Expect the unexpected and you will never be let down. Just work hard at what you are investing in and keep pushing toward new goals every moment you live. If something fabulous comes along that you did not expect, then you are doing alright. Enjoy the moment. If something awful comes around that you did not expect, what is the lesson in it? There's something you need to learn. Look at it and grow.

I can't help
but feel you all
around me.

Exit Stage Left

When I leave the stage
I pray that I inspired someone and gave them a reason
To keep moving forward in their life
I hope they heard my story and think, WOW
If she can make it, I can
I hope they can see that God lives in all of us
And that we are an extension of HIS LOVE
I hope they heard themselves in the songs
I hope they feel moved to tears and inspired to walk
Through all their fears and give back to themselves
But also to the world
I really hope they feel love and the love they deserve

When I leave this earth
I hope I have left behind a legacy of work
That moves from one generation to the next
I hope my pain and all my sacrifices didn't go in vain
I pray that I have done more than enough to inspire others
I pray that I have made my family and my friends proud
I pray that my Father, my God, is proud
I pray that my ancestors, those before me, feel
I have carried their torch well

When I leave the stage of life
I want to feel like I left nothing out
I want to know I loved, gave life, dreamt big, worked hard
And made a difference in the human race
I want to leave knowing I LIVED!

First Lady
Michelle Obama
knows who I am

I BELONG

There were so many beautiful women from different walks of life all around me. Just like the decor in the Grand East Room, which displayed a vibrant array of lavender, purple and red roses on pink tablecloths, Mrs. Obama had assembled all shades of beautiful women seated in their chairs like queens on thrones. She was not only celebrating accomplished women, but she was also spotlighting the importance of being a mentor.

I walked in feeling blessed and honored to be one of the chosen few to be a part of this evening. My heart pounded as I went to my seat, not noticing as I walked past a pool of press on my left. I was distracted by a delightful hug from Judith Jamison.

On the inside, I wanted to scream—I couldn't believe she knew who I was. Feeling like I used to feel on the first day of school, I searched for my seat and finally took a moment to take a deep breath. Two mentors were seated at each table with groups of teenagers about to graduate from high school. The

Faith and love and hard work,
those are the things that got
us all through. And that's
really all you need. You don't
need money. You don't need
connections. You just need
to work really hard and push
yourselves and push beyond
your fear, because fear is all a
part of it. We have all felt fear.
We've all felt doubt. But
the question is, Do you let
that stop you, or do you
keep pushing through?
—*Michelle Obama*

other mentor at my table was Rashida Jones, who I later discovered is the daughter of the great producer Quincy Jones. I had seen her on the television show *The Office* but didn't put it all together until the next day. Rashida and I did everything we could think of to lighten the mood for the girls surrounding us, such as cracking jokes and encouraging them to enjoy the moment. At the table we began conversations with these young women who were about to begin the next phase of their lives. We asked them to share their stories. Some had scars hidden behind smiles; some had plans; and some were just like me, amazed by the opportunities they were given every day.

Finally, the First Lady walked in with an inspired glow and a smile that made the sun look dim. She greeted us with laughter and excitement while glancing at her papers as she prepared to begin her speech. She spoke about three women who inspired her by their perseverance and courage to never give up on their dreams.

To my surprise, three days after my birthday, there I was at the White House having dinner with beautiful, distinguished women. As if that weren't enough, the most powerful woman in the world felt inspired enough to tell the world about my journey. I was one of the three women she spoke about. I had walked into the White House thinking no one knew who I was and no one cared. But the First Lady knew and made sure my story was told. I really wished my mother were sitting next to me. It was all I could do to hold back my tears. Mrs. Obama stopped in the middle of her speech to ask the audience to wish me a happy belated birthday.

I tell you, that almost knocked the wind out of me. Everyone applauded with smiles. I was so embarrassed. Mrs. Obama ended her speech as if she were watering a garden, inspiring us to never stop growing, to never stop dreaming and to always inspire others. Then she simply said, "Now we can eat!" I looked over to Rashida, who is a friend to this day. She made me laugh,

The First Lady knew and made sure my story was told. I really wished my mother were sitting next to me.

saying, "Go, Led, a shout-out from the First Lady!"

I love her for making me laugh rather than cry. It brought me back to enjoying the moment. I had begun to get too serious. At some point during the evening, I began remembering my past. I thought about the abuse I had endured, being molested and my mother being constantly beaten by my stepfather. I thought about being grateful for the Goodwill store and going to the library every Saturday with my mom and sister. I thought about sleeping on the floor with two suitcases, wondering if I was ever going to be a famous singer. I thought about the people who said, "You are nothing and you never will be!"

Yet there I was at the White House for the second time in one month.

I remember praying, asking God to let me one day meet the Obama family, but never thought I would actually be sitting there.

God gave me more than I could have ever expected. Since then, I have been at the White House a third time for the President's birthday. Each time, I have been inspired. I love how the Obamas love each other and how they love people.

At the end of the evening, I sang for all the women. The last song I sang was one I wrote titled "Alright." I wrote this song when I was ready to give up on my dream. I told the story behind the song and began to sing. Many of the women in the room began to cry. As I was getting close to the end, I asked everyone to sing along. That was the best feeling in the world, hearing every person in the East Room singing a song I wrote.

That feeling reminded me of my purpose and why I belonged in the company of such great women. I couldn't wait to call my mom.

That experience will be with me for the rest of my life.

My name is Peaches!

BLACK GIRLS ROCK

Everywhere I go, people ask me about my experience at Black Girls Rock, aired on BET. My appearance on that show changed my life forever. For the first time in my career, I decided I would no longer hide myself to make others feel comfortable. I always felt when I performed with other singers that I should sing less and not be myself so that they would feel comfortable enough to sing with me. I would always get so nervous when singing with others. Whenever I sang with the greats like Chaka, Patti and Rachelle Ferrell, they pushed me to sing more in a loving way. I remember reading Patti LaBelle's book *Don't Block the Blessings*. She spoke about hiding her gift so she could have friends, not singing full out to make others comfortable. That stuck with me for years, because I grew up haunted by those feelings. Every time I opened my mouth, it felt like a gift as well as a curse. A lot of attention would come my way, accompanied by jealousy and drama. I worried about how others would feel instead of just singing.

This time I decided I could not hide my gift. This song required that I sing the meaning of Peaches. Nina Simone wrote "Four Women" to describe four different black women. Peaches is strong, an angry fighter. Everything had to fit her character, from my movements, my vocal phrasing, my hair, makeup,

shoes and outfit. I studied Ms. Nina the whole week before the show, knowing I had to figure out how to give the voice of Peaches a new spin. I needed to add my voice to the equation. I studied Ms. Nina's movements, her phrasing and the way she held herself when she sang Peaches. By the time it was my turn to sing, I went to my position like a fighter who had trained for this moment and I was ready—we all were ready. The all-female band and the four performers onstage knew we were creating a historic moment. It would take all of us to make this moment special. The anticipation of it made me so nervous that honestly every time the music started during rehearsals, I felt like throwing up. The funny thing was, when I first sang my part in the rehearsal, I was afraid. I needed to hear my voice as Peaches; I needed to know if our voices had become one. After the first time I sang it, I was shaking and I knew this was going to be a powerful moment. It was so much bigger than me. This was about Nina Simone, and I wanted to please her. I wanted everyone to see and hear what I heard and envisioned for Peaches. I only had one shot to do it. I walked down the stairs in a long coat-gown with a high collar (specially designed for me), tight black jeans and high heels. My hair and makeup were exactly as I wanted. For the first time, I wasn't nervous. I was ready to tell Nina's story the way she wanted. I was ready to tell them, "My Name Is Peaches!"

This was about Nina Simone, and I wanted to please her.

Dreams
come
true

As much as I wanted to run from it, I was on my first headlining tour, selling out venues. One of my dreams had finally come true. One performance on the tour stood out the most for me. It was playing at the legendary Apollo Theater. Everything about that place has the energy of who I am, something old and something new. I flew Mom in to share the moment with me. I sang all her favorite songs—she especially loves "Knocking." She rocked with the crowd and I sang onstage. It was a wonderful night. I called out to Mom and told her to take a bow. This was our moment. My mom's chest was poked out like a peacock. She was so proud. After the show, she got the chance to rub the log. Yes, she rubbed the log enough for both of us. She always wanted to do that, but you had to be performing on the stage in order to do it. She was performing on that stage as far as I was concerned. Mom made all this happen for me by supporting my dream. She's been able to dream through me.

Mom, I love you.

All of this is your dream.

The people
who doubt
your ability
are fuel for
your success.

Pieces of Me

People just don't know what I'm about
They haven't seen what's there behind
  my smile
There's so much more of me I'm showing now
These are the pieces of me
When it looks like I'm up, sometimes I'm down
I'm alone even with people all around
But that don't change the happiness I found
These are the pieces of me

So when you look at my face
You gotta know that I'm made
Of everything love and pain
These are the pieces of me
Like every woman I know
I'm complicated fo' sho
But when I love
I love till there's no love no more
These are the pieces of me

So many colors
That make up the woman that you see
A good friend and lover
Anything you want, yes, I can be
I run the business and make time for fantasy
These are the pieces of me
Now I'm gonna make mistakes from time to time
But in the end believe that I'm gon' fly
No matter if I'm wrong or if I'm right
These are the pieces of me

So when you look at my face
You gotta know that I'm made
Of everything love and pain
These are the pieces of me
Like every woman I know
I'm complicated fo' sho
But when I love
I love till there's no love no more
These are the pieces of me

Oh, as the pieces of me start to unfold
Now I start to understand
All that I am
A woman not afraid to
Be strong, strong

So when you look at my face
You gotta know that I'm made
Of everything love and pain
These are the pieces of me
Like every woman I know
I'm complicated fo' sho
But when I love, I love till
There's no love no more
These are the pieces of me
I'm a woman, a woman, a woman
A woman, woman, woman, woman
Yes, I'm a woman, a woman
These are the pieces of me
—Ledisi Young, Claude Kelly and Chuck Harmony

Thinking of You

My name is Ledisi...
As the world turns
And the moon fades
And the sun begins to shine
Like the flowers and the trees grow
You're always on my mind
I can't help but feel you all around me
Feel you everywhere
Yeah! You bring me peace of mind
Peace of mind
You bring joy to my soul, yeah
Everywhere that I go
Every day, every night
I think of you
You're the air that I breathe
You're the love of my life
I think of you

Every second
Every hour
Till time runs out of time
Like a river
To a waterfall
I need you in my life
I can't help but
Feel you all around me
Feel you everywhere
Yeah! You bring me peace of mind
Peace of mind
You bring joy to my soul, yeah
Everywhere that I go
Every day, every night
I think of you
You're the air that I breathe
You're the love of my life
I think of you
—Ledisi Young and Rex Rideout

Papa Loved to Love Me

No, no, please don't
No, no, please don't
No, no, please don't

Verse
I remember it all like it was yesterday
I remember praying, Jesus, won't cha
  come my way
I remember the liquor on his breath
His hand on my thigh
I couldn't scream
All I did was cry
Why nobody saved me?
Why did God make me?
Blaming it all on myself
When I couldn't do nothing else, when

Chorus
Papa loved to love me
Nobody tried to save me
Papa loved to love me
Now I'm the one who's crazy, yeah
Papa loved to love me
Nobody tried to save me

Papa loved to love me
Now I'm the one who's crazy

Verse
When I told Mama, she went away
  that day
Something in her face will never be
  the same
I know she tried to save me
But soon I went crazy
Wondering why I had to fight him
  off me every night
Trying to keep the light
The light of my heaven, the light of
  my innocence
The light of my future, soon gaining
  the light of my strength
I'm older now not using that bruise
  as my excuse
One had to be strong to survive
  this abuse, when

(Chorus Out)

Now I'm free!
—Ledisi Young and Sundra Manning

Answer to Why

Why me? And how did I get here?
What now? And where do I go?
I'm so scared, life ever changing
And the pain, will it ever go?

Please let me breathe
I just wanna know the answer to why
Every day I breathe
I just wanna know the answer to why
In time, I will know the answer
Right now, I need to find a way
To let go of all my secrets
And embrace the sun on my face

So many questions I have
So many prayers left unanswered
There's always a blessing, still I am guessing
Finding my way through the dark

Every day I breathe
I just wanna know the answer to why
Every day I breathe
I just wanna know the answer to why
Every day I breathe
I just wanna know the answer to why
Every day I breathe
I just wanna know the answer to why

Oh, everything changes
I wanna know why
Oh, everything changes
Oh, everything changes

Every day I breathe
I just wanna know the answer to why

—Ledisi Young and Lorenzo Johnson

Simple

I can't stop the rain
But I can ease your pain for a little while
I can sing a song that would make you smile
I can do those things and more
But let me tell you, I can't save the world
But I can do the thing I am called to do
And I hope that it will inspire you
'Cause that's what love is for

That's what it's about
That's what it's about
As simple as it sounds
That's what it's about
Love will pull you out as simple as it sounds
That's what it's about
That's what it's about
As simple as it sounds
That's what it's about
That's what it's about
As simple as it sounds

Ain't no need for metaphors
To explain what we should explore
Don't you worry about what's next
Keep it simple, not so complex
Let me tell you that
Life never explains the why and when
Certain things are happening
There's a reason for everything
Just choose love to open the door
That's what it's about
That's what it's about
As simple as it sounds
That's what it's about

Love will pull you out as simple as it sounds
That's what it's about
That's what it's about
As simple as it sounds
That's what it's about
That's what it's about
As simple as it sounds

Hey! You know there's nothing more greater
  than love
It's a gift sent from heaven above
Throw your hands up, don't cha know, it's alright
Sometimes you gotta let it go
Hey, what I say to you, I tell you the truth
It's simple for me, it's simple for you
Hey, as easy as it sounds
That's what it's about

Simple! Simple! Simple
Simple as it sounds
Simple! Hey! Simple! Hey!
Simple! Hey! Simple! Hey!
Simple as it sounds (repeat)

That's what it's about
That's what it's about
As simple as it sounds
That's what it's about
Love will pull you out as simple as it sounds
That's what it's about
That's what it's about
As simple as it sounds
That's what it's about
That's what it's about
As simple as it sounds
—Ledisi Young and Rex Rideout

Photo Credits

Images by BunnyBootsPhotography
except where otherwise noted

Page 1: Derek Blanks
Page 3: Eric Levin
Page 8: Melanie Dunea

CHAPTER 1 – FAITH
Page 12: Sheila Prevost/SLPD Illustration
18: Lisa Spindler/Getty Images
23: Rita Maas/Getty Images

CHAPTER 2 – BEAUTY
Page 26: Marc Baptiste
30: Saddi Khali
32–33: Mark Lewis/Getty Images
37: Keith Mallet Illustration
38: Richard Maitland
39: Josh Olin/Trunk Archive

CHAPTER 3 – LOVE
Page 42: Adreinne Waheed
48: Jason Imber

CHAPTER 4 – SHINE
Page 57: John-Francis Bourke/Getty Images
58–59: Gregor Schuster/Getty Images
61: Lorenzo Johnson
64–65: Peggy Moore
67: Adreinne Waheed

CHAPTER 5 – AUTHENTIC
Page 70: Sheila Prevost/SLPD Illustration
75: Beth Herzhaft
78: Eyebeam Photography/Getty Images
81: Imagno/Getty Images

CHAPTER 6 – BELIEVE
Page 84: Sheila Prevost/SLPD Illustration
87: Marie Dalton
88: New York Daily News Archive/Getty Images

CHAPTER 7 – FORGIVENESS
Page 94: Asharkyu/Shutterstock
97: Annie Griffiths Belt/Corbis
98–99: Stuart McClymont/Getty Images
103: Adreinne Waheed

CHAPTER 8 – TREASURES
Page 112: Photofest
116–117: Charles Ommanney/Contour by Getty Images
120–121: Carol Whaley Addassi/Getty Images
123: Eve Arnold/Magnum Photos
127: Echoes/Redferns/Getty Images

CHAPTER 9 – ALRIGHT
Page 130: Derek Blanks
132: Adrian Boot/urbanimage.tv
135: Derek Blanks

CHAPTER 10 – HOME
Page 141: Young Family
142: NyDy (Mama in 9th grade)
143: Young Family; Ti Curry (Mama at 14)
144: Young Family
147: Young Family
152: Chad Kleitsch/Getty Images
(also appears on cover)

CHAPTER 11 – TAKE A BOW
Page 156: Caspar Benson/Getty Images
163: Kwaku Alston/Corbis Outline
165: Chip Somodevilla/Getty Images
167: Brad Barket/AP Photo

Back Cover: Derek Blanks

Images are the copyright of the artist/photographer